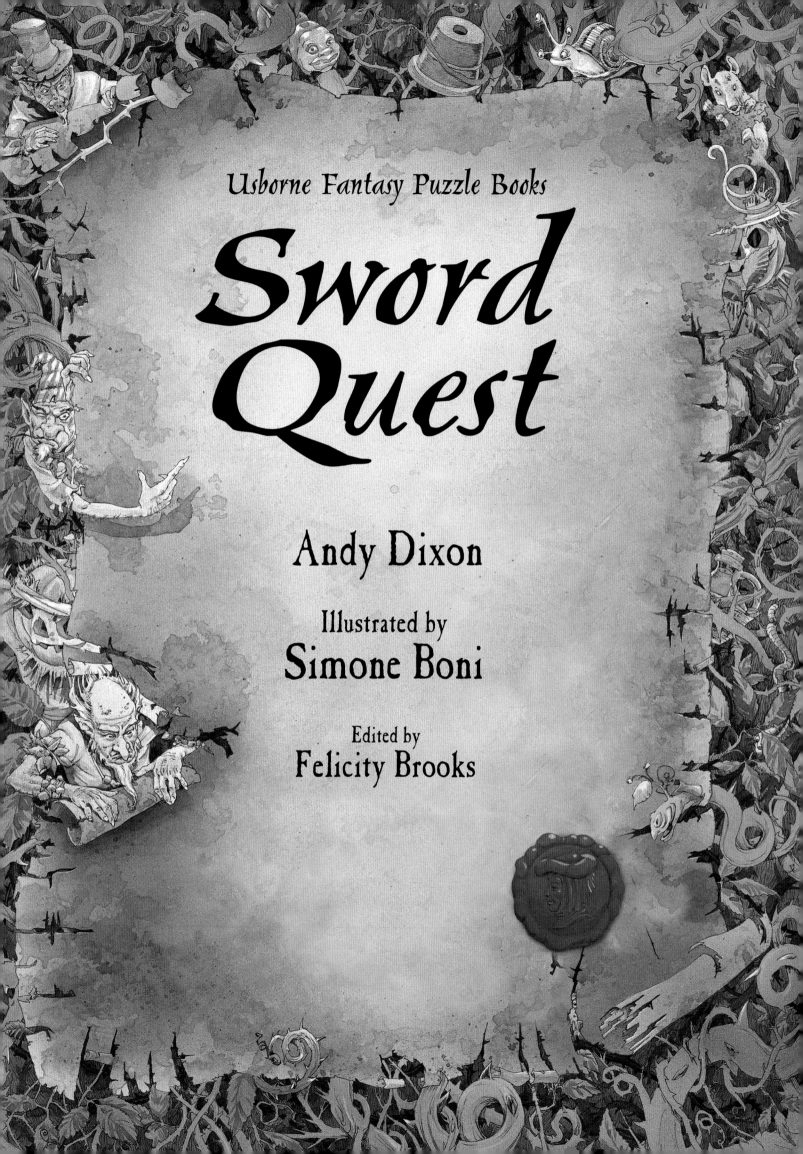

Usborne Fantasy Puzzle Books

Sword
Quest

Andy Dixon

Illustrated by
Simone Boni

Edited by
Felicity Brooks

Cover and additional design by
Stephanie Jones and Keith Newell
Additional editing by Claire Masset

This edition first published in 2010 by Usborne Publishing Ltd, 83–85 Saffron Hill, London EC1N 8RT, England.
Copyright © 2010, 2005, 1997 Usborne Publishing Ltd.
UE. Printed in China. First published in America 2010.

Good Citizens of Gladlands,

I bring you bad tidings of great woe. A terrible calamity has befallen our kingdom – the sacred Sword of Glee has been taken from us; stolen by the evil, shape-changing villain, Blag the Untrustworthy! Disguised as our good king, Blag crept into Castle Glee and tricked Muddle the Magician, the keeper of the sword, into handing it over. But that nasty creature Blag did not stop there. Using the sword's great power for his own evil ends, he kidnapped the real king, Gilbert the Gracious, and now holds him prisoner in Castle Gloom on the far side of Gladlands.

I have just received a ransom note from Blag demanding that we all go to work as his slaves in the Fields of Fancy, growing crops for his armies so that they may grow ever stronger. If we do not submit to his evil plan, we will never see Gilbert again!

The time has come to put a stop to Blag's wicked ways. I call upon all Gladlanders to compete in a tournament at Castle Glee to find the bravest, strongest and wisest amongst us to defeat Blag, and return the king and the sword to their rightful home. So, good citizens, I am looking for:

VOLUNTEERS TO GO ON THE SWORD QUEST

Will you be one of the chosen few? Come to the tournament and find out.

By order of

Gladys the Glamorous

(The king's grandmother)

Important information for all questers

Thank you for volunteering to go on the Sword Quest, and welcome to Gladlands. There are some things you need to know before you set off.

Where am I?

You are at Castle Glee in Gladlands where a terrible calamity has struck the royal family.

Oh dear! What happened?

An evil, shape-changing villain, named Blag the Untrustworthy, has kidnapped Gilbert the Gracious, Gladland's rightful ruler, and is holding him prisoner in Castle Gloom. Blag has also stolen the sacred Sword of Glee which is the source of all Gilbert's power.

Oh no! Anything else I should know?

Yes indeed. Blag has sent Gilbert's granny, Gladys the Glamorous, a ransom note, demanding that all Gladlanders work as his slaves in the Fields of Fancy. If they refuse they will never see Gilbert again.

So what can I do about it?

Go on the quest to Castle Gloom to rescue King Gilbert, defeat Blag the Untrustworthy and bring the magic sword and the king back to Castle Glee.

Who'll go with me?

Gladys has organized a grand tournament at Castle Glee. The three winners will go with you on the Sword Quest. The tournament is starting soon.

How much time do we have?

Not long. Every day that Blag has the magic sword his evil powers grow stronger. Your mission must be accomplished as quickly as possible.

How do we get to Castle Gloom?

You'll set out from Castle Glee and travel through Gladlands. The map below shows the whole of Gladlands. Please study it carefully.

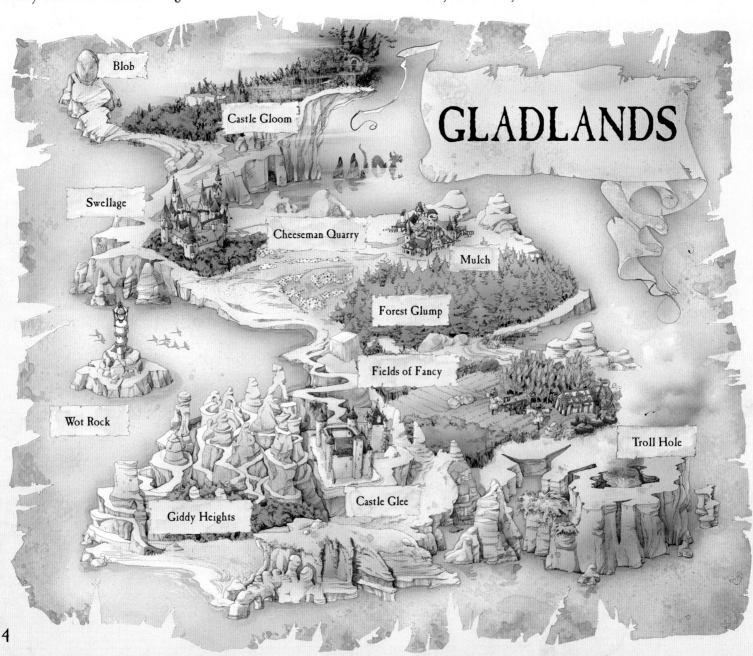

Blob

Castle Gloom

GLADLANDS

Swellage

Cheeseman Quarry

Mulch

Forest Glump

Fields of Fancy

Wot Rock

Troll Hole

Castle Glee

Giddy Heights

The parchments

The quest will be both difficult and dangerous, so you will need courage, cunning and the eyes of an eagle if you are to survive. In every place you visit you will see a piece of parchment similar to the one below. It contains vital information to get you safely through to the next stage of the quest.

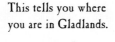

SAMPLE

The boat is a magical place. It is small on the outside, but enormous inside, and it's full of toys that the old sailor collected on his travels around the world. He also used it as a workshop to make wonderful new toys. You must find out how the boat works before you can continue your journey.

Somewhere there is a clockwork sailor who steers the boat. He will only work when he is wearing his sailor's hat and is wound up with a special key. If you can find the sailor, the hat and the key, you can begin your boat trip.

There are some model castles on the boat. To make the clockwork sailor steer the boat in the right direction, find the model that looks like Castle Gloom (before Blag let it go to wrack and ruin) and place it in the direction finder.

In the engine room, on the lower deck, a clockwork man stokes the furnace with coal. To get the boat moving you need to find 7 lumps of coal for him.

There are many pies in the boat, but only four of them are real. The others are toys. Find 4 real pies.

This tells you where you are in Gladlands.

These maps will help to remind you where each place is in Gladlands. They come from a collection of maps owned by Muddle the Magician of Castle Glee.

When it is time, read these pieces of information carefully. They contain some very important clues.

The pictures show people or things you have to find or avoid in each place you visit. Some will be very hard to spot, because you can only see a small part of them.

Some pictures show things you will need later in the quest or ways of getting to the next place.

At the bottom of the parchment are pictures of food or drink to look for. You can find something to eat in each place you visit.

The squares

At the bottom of each page are some more pictures in squares. The numbers tell you how many of that thing you can spot in the main scene. Finding these things will sharpen your skills and help you to survive the quest.

5 jack-in-the-boxes

10 tin soldiers

Your enemy, Blag the Untrustworthy, holding the sacred Sword of Glee.

You can recognize Blag from his one white eye, which he cannot change.

Blag's eye

Blag the Untrustworthy is a master of disguise and can change himself into anything he wants to be, but one thing always gives him away: he has one white eye which he cannot change. Keep a lookout for him in each place you visit, because he may be hiding, getting ready to trick you.

The gemstones

Hidden in each of the first ten places you visit is one gemstone. You will need all ten later to help you defeat Blag, so don't forget to look for them.

The Castle Glee tournament is about to begin. Turn the page to find out who will be going with you on the SWORD QUEST...

Castle Glee

Welcome to the Tournament of Knighthood at Castle Glee. Gladys the Glamorous is busy looking for the three people with enough courage, cunning and skill to go with you on the quest to retrieve the Sword of Glee. Can you find the ones she's chosen in the crowd?

Sir Loin du Stake is an elderly knight with a rusty sword and shield. He wears a monocle in his right eye.

Lady Egg wears an orange three pointed hat. She has a beauty spot above her lip.

Tern the Page wears one green shoe and one brown shoe, and takes his pet woffit with him wherever he goes.

Castle Gloom is far away. You will need to travel there on quockback. Can you find 4 quocks?

You'll be very hungry after the tournament. Find 20 assorted cakes, and a fish sandwich to eat.

9 woffits

5 drums

7 sticky sticks

7 rattles   4 abacuses   5 goblets   10 red noses   10 stingers

Magic Workshop

You have been called into Muddle the Magician's workshop so that he and Gladys can give you some vital equipment and information for your quest. When you arrive you find that one of Muddle's magic spells has gone wrong. Everything is floating around the room.

First find the butterfly net and catch the Spellbook, so that you can reverse the spell. It will then take a day or so for the magic to wear off. Take the Spellbook with you on your journey.

You will need a map of Gladlands to help you reach Castle Gloom. Find the map holder.

Gladys has brought the ancient weapons of Glee for you to take on your journey. There are 4 sharp swords and 4 shields to find.

Good food and drink is very important on a long journey. Find 12 crabby apples and 6 water bags.

13 potion bottles	6 dividers	7 pestles

5 microscopes

8 quills

17 lizards

6 pairs of spectacles

9 crystal balls

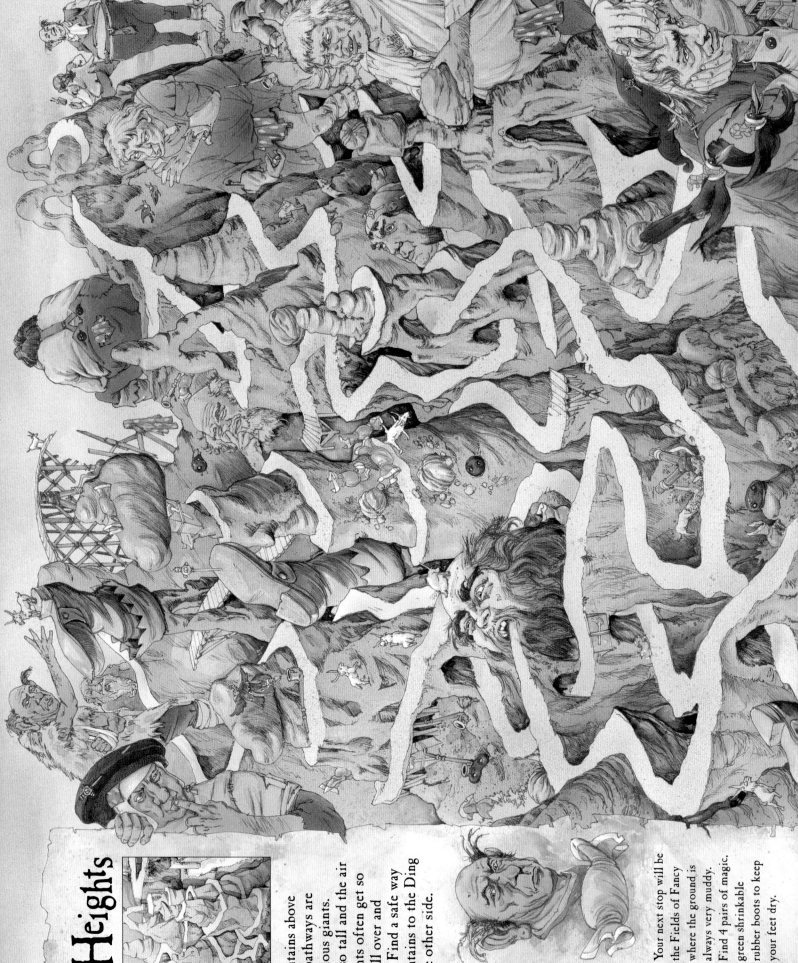

Giddy Heights

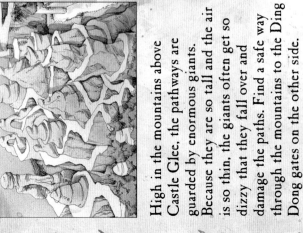

High in the mountains above Castle Glee, the pathways are guarded by enormous giants. Because they are so tall and the air is so thin, the giants often get so dizzy that they fall over and damage the paths. Find a safe way through the mountains to the Ding Dong gates on the other side.

To pass the giants safely, give each of them a mint to suck to stop their ears from popping when they stand up. There are 17 giants and 17 mints to find.

Your next stop will be the Fields of Fancy where the ground is always very muddy. Find 4 pairs of magic, green shrinkable rubber boots to keep your feet dry.

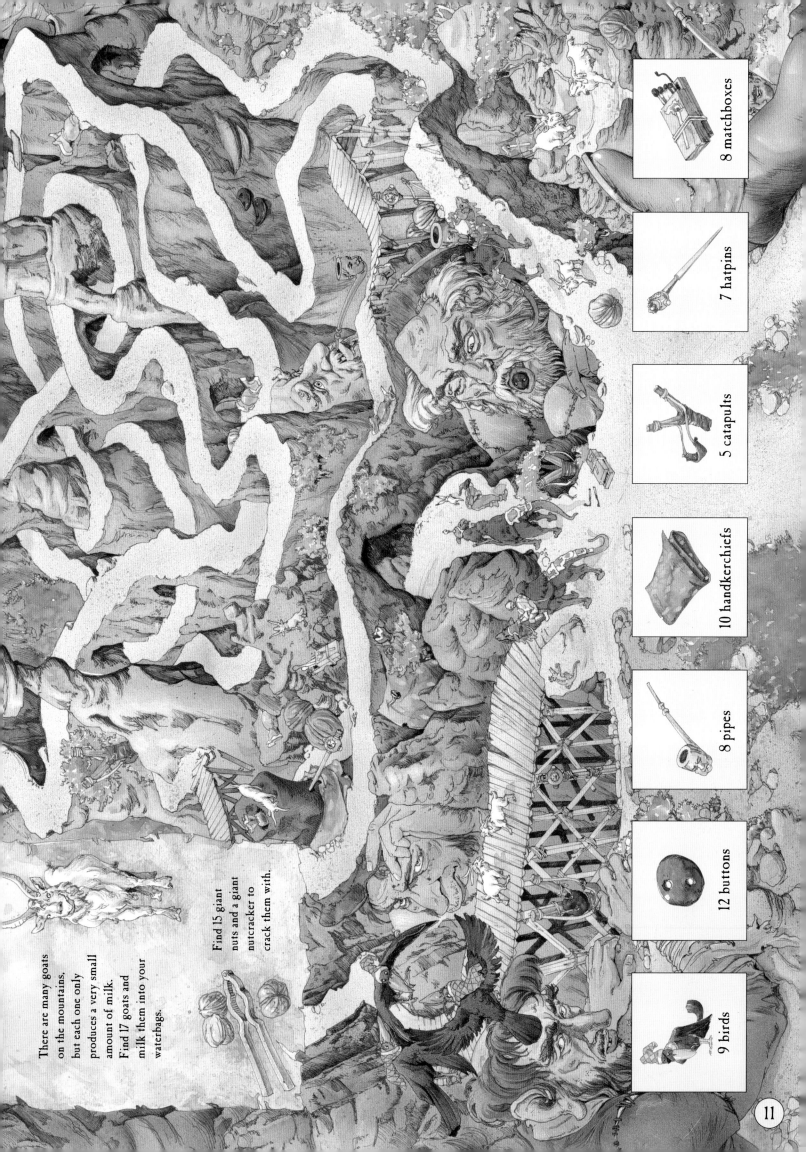

There are many goats on the mountains, but each one only produces a very small amount of milk. Find 17 goats and milk them into your waterbags.

Find 15 giant nuts and a giant nutcracker to crack them with.

8 matchboxes

7 hatpins

5 catapults

10 handkerchiefs

8 pipes

12 buttons

9 birds

Fields of Fancy

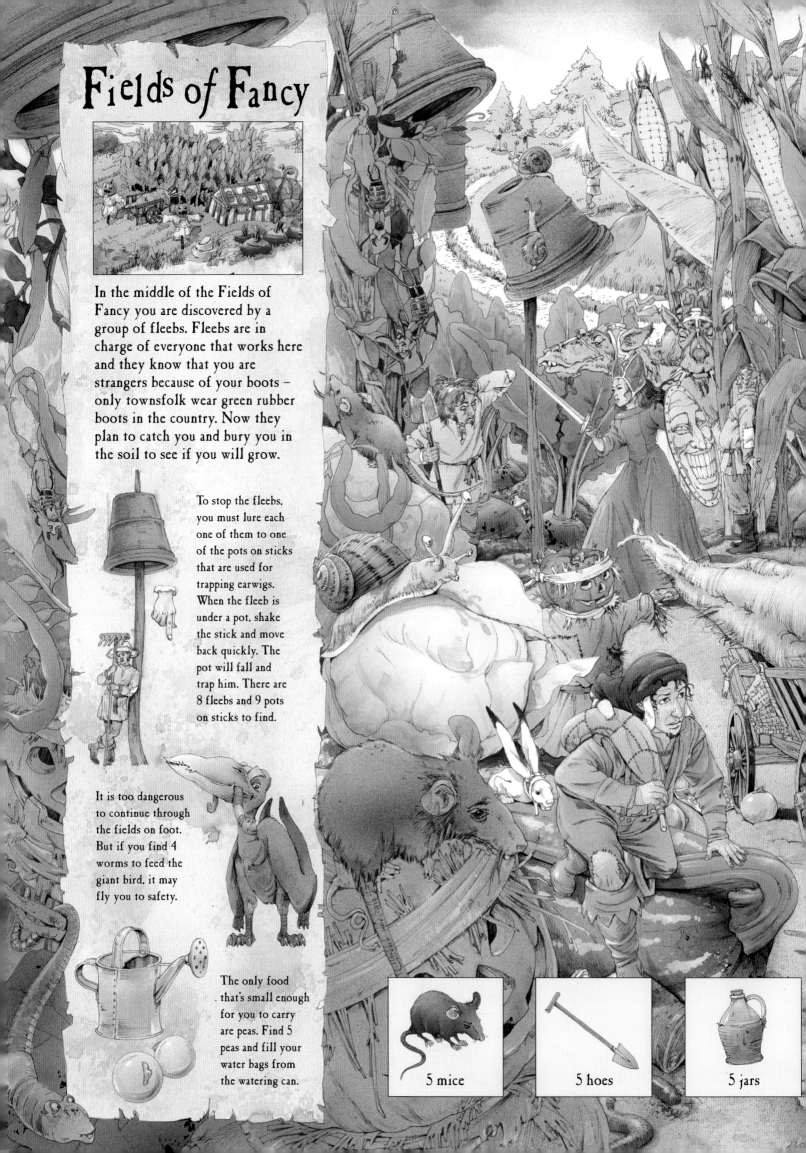

In the middle of the Fields of Fancy you are discovered by a group of fleebs. Fleebs are in charge of everyone that works here and they know that you are strangers because of your boots – only townsfolk wear green rubber boots in the country. Now they plan to catch you and bury you in the soil to see if you will grow.

To stop the fleebs, you must lure each one of them to one of the pots on sticks that are used for trapping earwigs. When the fleeb is under a pot, shake the stick and move back quickly. The pot will fall and trap him. There are 8 fleebs and 9 pots on sticks to find.

It is too dangerous to continue through the fields on foot. But if you find 4 worms to feed the giant bird, it may fly you to safety.

The only food that's small enough for you to carry are peas. Find 5 peas and fill your water bags from the watering can.

5 mice

5 hoes

5 jars

8 snails   6 scarecrows   3 spray cans   5 packets of seeds   9 earwigs

Mulch Market

The giant bird has dropped you in the town of Mulch. Every day is market day in Mulch, so it's always full of strange people and weird creatures. It's an extremely dirty, smelly and noisy place to be. You're still a long way from Castle Gloom. You need to find some way of getting there.

If you can get hold of a boat, you can sail all the way to Castle Gloom on the river that runs through Mulch. Sir Loin has found out that there's a sailor in the town who'll give you a boat in return for some glugs. The old man has always dreamed of starting his own glug farm. Find 11 baby glugs and the sailor.

A glug

Some of Blag's soldiers are in town. They have orders to capture any strangers. Spot all eight, so you can avoid them.

No one uses money in Mulch. People just exchange things. To get something to eat, find 4 green umbrellas and exchange them for some food.

7 clothears

5 quock droppings

7 plants

3 sacks of grain

8 giant grubs

11 cluck eggs

3 wheelbarrows

9 trunkbills

Magic Boat

The boat is a magical place. It is small on the outside, but enormous inside, and it's full of toys that the old sailor collected on his travels around the world. He also used it as a workshop to create wonderful new toys. You must find out how the boat works before you can continue your journey.

Somewhere there is a clockwork sailor who steers the boat. He will only work when he is wearing his sailor's hat and is wound up with a special key. If you can find the sailor, the hat and the key, you can begin your boat trip.

There are some model castles on the boat. To make the clockwork sailor steer the boat in the right direction, find the model that looks like Castle Gloom (before Blag let it go to wrack and ruin) and place it in the direction finder.

In the engine room, on the lower deck, a clockwork man stokes the furnace with coal. To get the boat moving you need to find 7 lumps of coal for him.

There are many pies in the boat, but only four of them are real. The others are toys. Find 4 real pies.

5 jack-in-the-boxes

3 silly masks

10 tin soldiers

7 hoppers   6 fishmobiles   10 cuddly toys   4 flying machines   7 baby dolls

Swellheads

The boat has drifted into a small town where the Swellheads live. The Swellheads are very clever and have very big heads to make room for their very big brains. They are only interested in things that will improve their knowledge, but they seem fairly friendly.

The Swellheads would like to study your boat, but this will take them a very long time. (It takes them a very long time to do anything.) You don't have time to spare, so you need to exchange your boat for another. Can you find a punt and a pole?

It will soon be dark, so you will need to find something to light your way. Find a lamp and a bottle of lamp fuel.

Swellheads are usually so busy that they forget to eat. You will have to help yourselves to whatever half-eaten food they have left lying around. Find 4 forgotten fruit pies and 5 lost bottles of lemonade.

The Swellheads have mislaid the handle that opens the lock gates on the canal. You have to find the handle to continue your journey.

9 teapots

12 red books

18 monkeys

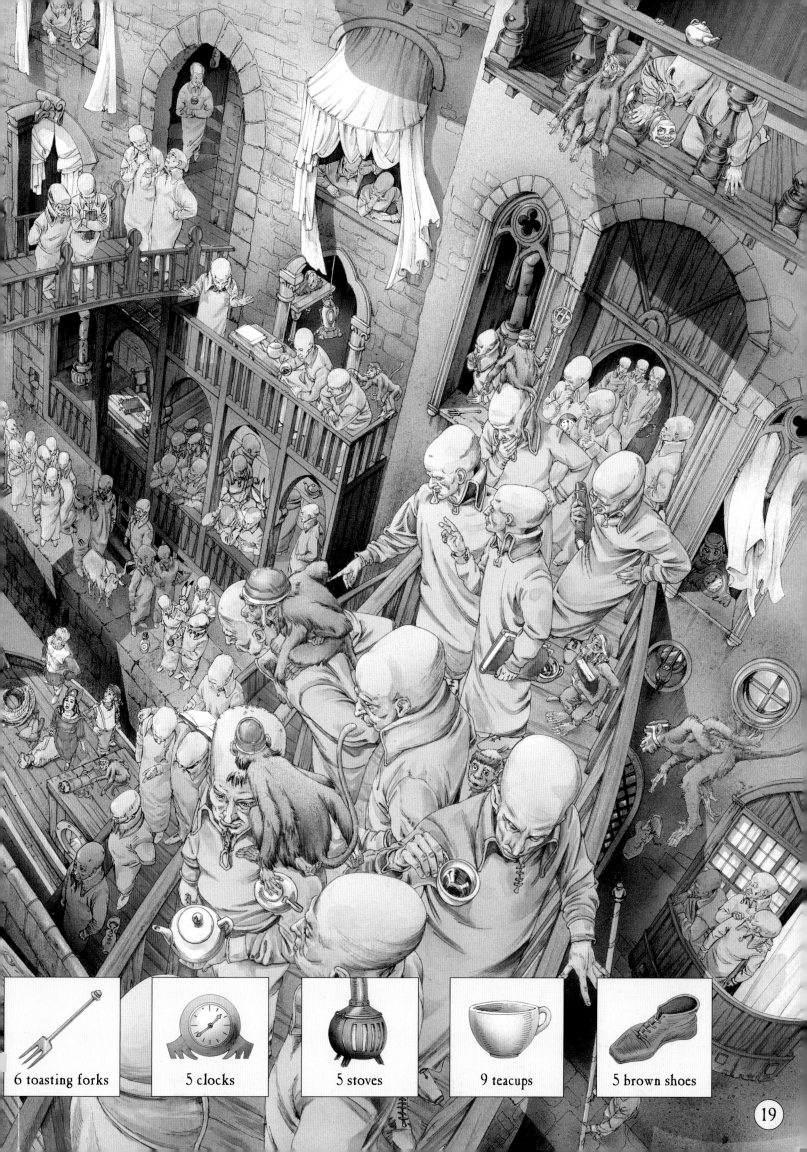

6 toasting forks
5 clocks
5 stoves
9 teacups
5 brown shoes

The Delves

The river runs through a forest where you are captured by delves. Delves are nasty pointy creatures who steal things from others. They have just stolen your boat and all your weapons, but they will let you go unharmed if you do something to help them.

The delves' machine for carrying water from the river to the treetops is broken. One of the cogs is missing. If you can find the cog, the delves will help you get to Castle Gloom.

There is a blind delve who knows about a secret underground tunnel which leads right to the heart of Castle Gloom. He wears dark glasses and carries a stick like this one. Can you find him?

The blind delve says the entrance to the tunnel is in the side of a hollow tree. Can you spot it?

There is no food in the tunnel. You will need to find 8 roasted cluck legs for the journey.

9 owls

7 stinger nests

11 ladders

8 moths   8 torches   6 concertinas   6 buckets   6 knives

Clown Dungeon

You have been betrayed! The blind delve was really Blag in disguise. He has thrown you into the Clown Dungeon in Castle Gloom, where King Gilbert the Gracious is also being held prisoner. Now you are standing on a rotating platform, surrounded by rows of stone carvings and some very hungry crocodiles.

The platform is turning so fast, you are in danger of being thrown into the crocodile pit. To stop the platform, find the hand on the clown statue that is different in some way, and twist it clockwise.

Now you must find a copy of the clown's face among the row of snake carvings and push its red nose with one of your pointing sticks.

Pointing stick

The platform will then rise to the next level where you must find the clown's face again and push its nose. If you do this quickly on each of the 5 levels, the platform will raise you out of the dungeon. But if you are too slow, it will sink and you will be eaten by the crocodiles.

The crocodiles get fed with fish once a day, but they prefer to eat people. There are lots of spare fish for you to eat if you can catch them with your pointing sticks.

5 forks

14 frogs

11 watches

18 starfish   8 cheeses   5 padlocks   13 skulls   6 loaves

The Great Hall

After escaping from the dungeon, you find yourselves in the Great Hall of Castle Gloom where Blag's personal guard of Grunts are eating. Grunts are the most smelly, filthy creatures in the whole world. Their smell is so bad, no one can stand being near them long enough to defeat them.

Grunts are afraid of only one thing – being clean. If you can find the fire hose and hydrant to spray the Grunts with water, they will run away.

It would take forever to find the sword in Castle Gloom's hundreds of rooms and secret passages. The only way to track it down is to follow Blag. He is disguised as one of the Grunts, but you can recognize him by his one white eye. Find Blag and follow him.

You will need plenty of energy if you are going to defeat Blag. Gather up all the food you can. There are 13 slices of stinky pizza and 4 jugs of jungle juice to find.

7 dominoes

6 plates

9 rats

5 glasses   6 woodworms   6 oil paintings   12 candles   8 shields

The Ramparts

You have followed Blag up to the very top of Castle Gloom. Using the power of the magic sword, he has brought all the stone carvings, called gargoyles, to life. The gargoyles are very nasty. They will bite you and throw you off the top of the castle unless you stop them.

You should have already found 10 magic gemstones on your travels. If you throw one gemstone into each of the gargoyles' mouths, the spell will be broken and they will turn to stone again.

Using the power of the sword, Blag has created a magic ball that protects him from your weapons. The only way to fight magic is with stronger magic. In the Spellbook there is one spell which is powerful enough to defeat Blag. Collect all the ingredients, follow the spell, and Blag will vanish forever.

Of all the spells inside this book, this one deserves a second look. It will destroy all evil powers (especially magic balls on towers). Put *3 red leaves* into a cup, and with *a pencil* mash them up. Collect *5 spiders* from the wall. Into the cup they all must fall. Now take *2 feathers* from a nest and find *the grub that's dressed the best*. Then mix them slowly one and all and throw them at the magic ball.

To be magically transported home, find the clocktower and the key to open its door. Step inside, put your hands on the sword and say this spell:

"Hands of time – it's half past three,
And time we went to Castle Glee,
Our quest is done, and we have won,
The king and sword are free!
(Hurrah!)"

7 clock springs

8 hammers

3 raverbird eggs

10 raverbirds   8 bent nails   6 chimneys   8 nests

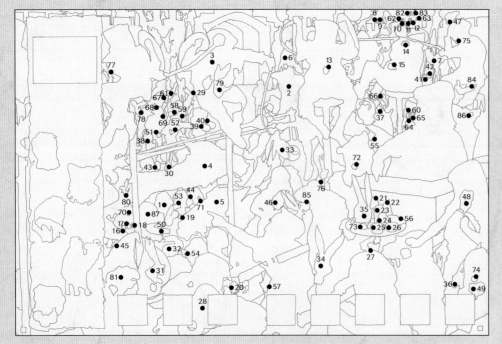

Castle Glee 6–7

Sir Loin 1

Lady Egg 2

Tern the Page 3

Quocks 4 5 6 7

Cakes 8 9 10 11 12 13 14 15 16 17 18 19 20 21 22 23 24 25 26 27

Fish sandwich 28

Woffits 29 30 31 32 33 34 35 36 37

Drums 38 39 40 41 42

Sticky sticks 43 44 45 46 47 48 49

Rattles 50 51 52 53 54 55 56

Abacuses 57 58 59 60

Goblets 61 62 63 64 65

Red noses 66 67 68 69 70 71 72 73 74 75

Stingers 76 77 78 79 80 81 82 83 84 85

Gem 86

Blag 87

Magic Workshop 8–9

Net 1

Spellbook 2

Map holder 3

Swords 4 5 6 7

Shields 8 9 10 11

Crabby apples 12 13 14 15 16 17 18 19 20 21 22 23

Water bags 24 25 26 27 28 29

Potion bottles 30 31 32 33 34 35 36 37 38 39 40 41 42

Dividers 43 44 45 46 47 48

Pestles 49 50 51 52 53 54 55

Microscopes 56 57 58 59 60

Quills 61 62 63 64 65 66 67 68

Lizards 69 70 71 72 73 74 75 76 77 78 79 80 81 82 83 84 85

Spectacles 86 87 88 89 90 91

Crystal balls 92 93 94 95 96 97 98 99 100

Gem 101

Blag 102

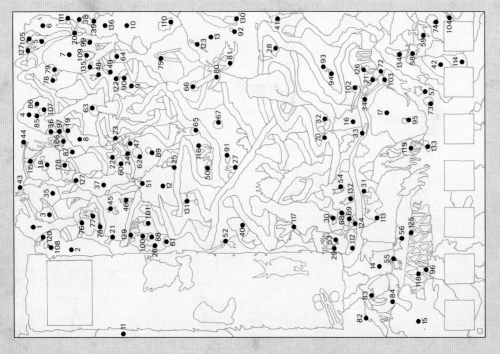

Giddy Heights 10–11

Giants 1 2 3 4 5 6 7 8 9 10 11 12 13 14 15 16 17

Mints 18 19 20 21 22 23 24 25 26 27 28 29 30 31 32 33 34

Boots 35 36 37 38 39 40 41 42

Goats 43 44 45 46 47 48 49 50 51 52 53 54 55 56 57 58 59

Nuts 60 61 62 63 64 65 66 67 68 69 70 71 72 73 74

Nutcracker 75

Birds 76 77 78 79 80 81 82 83 84

Buttons 85 86 87 88 89 90 91 92 93 94 95 96

Pipes 97 98 99 100 101 102 103 104

Handkerchiefs 105 106 107 108 109 110 111 112 113 114

Catapults 115 116 117 118 119

Hatpins 120 121 122 123 124 125 126

Matchboxes 127 128 129 130 131 132 133 134

Gem 135

Blag 136

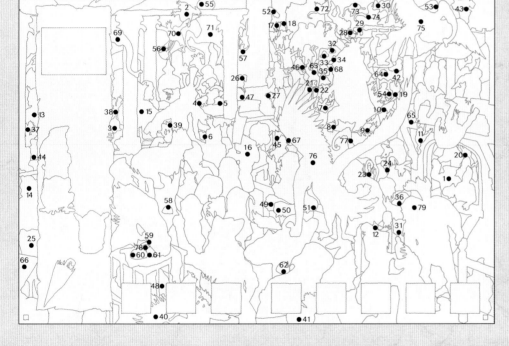

Fields of Fancy 12–13

Fleebs 1 2 3 4 5 6 7 8

Flowerpots 9 10 11 12 13 14 15 16 17

Bird 18

Worms 19 20 21 22

Watering can 23

Peas 24 25 26 27 28

Mice 29 30 31 32 33

Hoes 34 35 36 37 38

Jars 39 40 41 42 43

Snails 44 45 46 47 48 49 50 51

Scarecrows 52 53 54 55 56 57

Spray cans 58 59 60

Packets of seeds 61 62 63 64 65

Earwigs 66 67 68 69 70 71 72 73 74

Gem 75

Blag 76

Mulch Market 14–15

Sailor 1

Glugs 2 3 4 5 6 7 8 9 10 11 12

Soldiers 13 14 15 16 17 18 19 20

Green umbrellas 21 22 23 24

Clothears 25 26 27 28 29 30 31

Quock droppings 32 33 34 35 36

Plants 37 38 39 40 41 42 43

Sacks of grain 44 45 46

Giant grubs 47 48 49 50 51 52 53 54

Cluck eggs 55 56 57 58 59 60 61 62 63 64 65

Wheelbarrows 66 67 68

Trunkbills 69 70 71 72 73 74 75 76 77

Gem 78

Blag 79

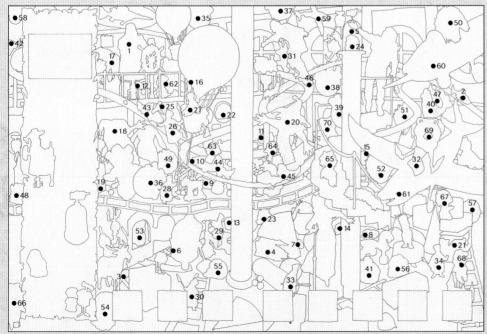

Magic Boat 16–17

Sailor 1

Hat 2

Key 3

Castle model 4

Direction finder 5

Lumps of coal 6 7 8 9 10 11 12

Real pies 13 14 15 16

Jack-in-the-boxes 17 18 19 20 21

Silly masks 22 23 24

Tin soldiers 25 26 27 28 29 30 31 32 33 34

Hoppers 35 36 37 38 39 40 41

Fishmobiles 42 43 44 45 46 47

Cuddly toys 48 49 50 51 52 53 54 55 56 57

Flying machines 58 59 60 61

Baby dolls 62 63 64 65 66 67 68

Gem 69

Blag 70

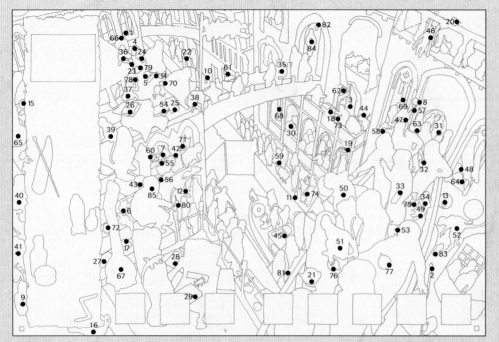

The Swellheads 18-19

Punt 1

Pole 2

Lamp 3

Lamp fuel 4

Fruit pies 5 6 7 8

Bottles of lemonade 9 10 11 12 13

Lock handle 14

Teapots 15 16 17 18 19 20 21 22 23

Red books 24 25 26 27 28 29 30 31 32 33 34 35

Monkeys 36 37 38 39 40 41 42 43 44 45 46 47 48 49 50 51 52 53

Forks 54 55 56 57 58 59

Clocks 60 61 62 63 64

Stoves 65 66 67 68 69

Teacups 70 71 72 73 74 75 76 77 78

Brown shoes 79 80 81 82 83

Gem 84

Blag 85

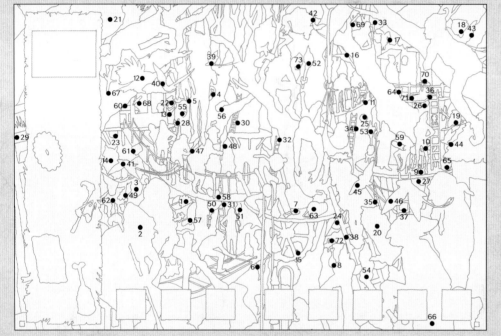

The Delves 20-21

Cog 1

Blind delve 2

Hollow tree 3

Roasted cluck legs 4 5 6 7 8 9 10 11

Owls 12 13 14 15 16 17 18 19 20

Stinger nests 21 22 23 24 25 26 27

Ladders 28 29 30 31 32 33 34 35 36 37 38

Moths 39 40 41 42 43 44 45 46

Torches 47 48 49 50 51 52 53 54

Concertinas 55 56 57 58 59 60

Buckets 61 62 63 64 65 66

Knives 67 68 69 70 71 72

Gem 73

Clown Dungeon 22-23

Clown faces 1 2 3 4 5

Hand that's different 6

Forks 7 8 9 10 11

Frogs 12 13 14 15 16 17 18 19 20 21 22 23 24 25

Watches 26 27 28 29 30 31 32 33 34 35 36

Starfish 37 38 39 40 41 42 43 44 45 46 47 48 49 50 51 52 53 54

Cheeses 55 56 57 58 59 60 61 62

Padlocks 63 64 65 66 67

Skulls 68 69 70 71 72 73 74 75 76 77 78 79 80

Loaves 81 82 83 84 85 86

Gem 87

Blag 88

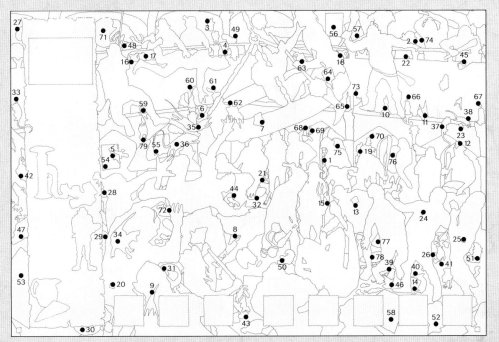

The Great Hall 24-25

Hose and hydrant 1

Blag 2

Slices of pizza 3 4 5 6 7 8 9 10 11 12 13 14 15

Jugs of jungle juice 16 17 18 19

Dominoes 20 21 22 23 24 25 26

Plates 27 28 29 30 31 32

Rats 33 34 35 36 37 38 39 40 41

Glasses 42 43 44 45 46

Woodworms 47 48 49 50 51 52

Oil paintings 53 54 55 56 57 58

Candles 59 60 61 62 63 64 65 66 67 68 69 70

Shields 71 72 73 74 75 76 77 78

Gems 79

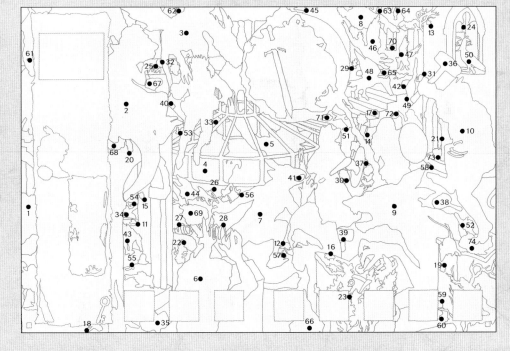

The Ramparts 26-27

Gargoyles 1 2 3 4 5 6 7 8 9 10

Red leaves 11 12 13

Pencil 14

Spiders 15 16 17 18 19

Feathers 20 21

Well-dressed grub 22

Key to clock tower 23

Clock tower 24

Clock springs 25 26 27 28 29 30 31

Hammers 32 33 34 35 36 37 38 39

Raverbird eggs 40 41 42

Raverbirds 43 44 45 46 47 48 49 50 51 52

Bent nails 53 54 55 56 57 58 59 60

Chimneys 61 62 63 64 65 66

Nests 67 68 69 70 71 72 73 74

Did you also notice?

~ five tiny men stealing cakes in Castle Glee?

~ a light bulb in the Magic Workshop?

~ a giant picking his nose in Giddy Heights?

~ a game of snakes and ladders in the Magic Boat?

~ a rat sitting on someone's head in the Great Hall?

~ a miserable earwig and a frightened giant grub in the Dungeon?

~ a toy pie in the Dungeon?

~ a toy pie in the Great Hall?

~ 3 skulls among the Delves?

~ 2 pigs, a lizard and a goat among the Delves?

~ an imprisoned goat in the Dungeon?

~ a crocodile that could be Blag in the Dungeon?

Goodbye!